by Lisa Cofield
and Debbie Dingerson

Cover Illustration by Design Dynamics, Glen Ellyn, IL
Typography by Roy Honegger

Published by Great Quotations Publishing Co.,
Glendale Heights, IL

Library of Congress Catalog Card Number: 95-81329

ISBN 1-56245-227-4

Printed in Hong Kong

To our parents, who tolerated us
when they didn't find us funny.

Introduction

Thousands of years ago, a Greek named Aesop travelled the countryside telling stories. His wife, Mrs. Aesop, realized that he wasn't the only one in the family wearing a toga, and decided to write some stories of her own. Unfortunately, her stories were lost over the years, while Mr. Aesop's fables went on to achieve the the fame and recognition they have today.

After lying undiscovered in the ruins for centuries, the stories of Mrs. Aesop have finally surfaced. The authors are honored to bring her stories to the public.

The Man and the Lion

One day Mr. Aesop told a story in his village. It was about a man and a Lion who travelled together through the forest. They soon began to boast of their respective superiority to each other in strength and prowess.

As they were disputing, they passed a statue carved in stone, which represented "a Lion strangled by a Man." The man pointed to it and said, "See there! How strong we are, and how we prevail over even the king of beasts." The Lion replied, "This statue was made by a man. If we Lions knew how to erect statues, you would see the Man placed under the paw of the Lion."

The next day, Mrs. Aesop began writing her own stories. "You can't write stories," said Mr. Aesop. "You know that men tell the best stories."

"Yes, dear," replied Mrs. Aesop with a knowing smile. "But that's only because until now, the men have told all the stories."

Moral: Sometimes the best version of history is herstory.

The Tortoise and the Hare

A Tortoise and a Hare once had a bet to see who could shed 20 pounds first. Ms. Hare joined a gym and did power aerobics three times a day. Meanwhile, Ms. Tortoise embarked on a steady program of daily walking.

After three days, Ms. Hare was half-way to her goal and was flaunting her new body to everyone in the gym. Ms. Tortoise, who had only lost two pounds, was taking it in stride.

After a week, though, Ms. Hare blew out her knee, had to have surgery and ended up gaining fifteen pounds because of the hospital food.

Ms. Tortoise, on the other hand, lost 20 pounds, won the bet, eloped with her personal trainer and lived happily ever after.

Moral: Slow and steady wins the race.

The Rooster and the Jewel

One bright day, a Rooster was scratching in the straw in his barnyard. The Rooster (male, by definition) was looking for food for his flock of hens, not realizing that the hens had been fending for themselves for years and were perfectly capable of finding their own food. But, roosters being roosters, the hens kindly let him believe he was indispensable.

As he scratched around, his claws turned up a 4-carat diamond. It was quite a rock! Any one of the hens would have given her first laid egg for the beautiful jewel.

"I'm sure this jewel is valuable, but I'm looking

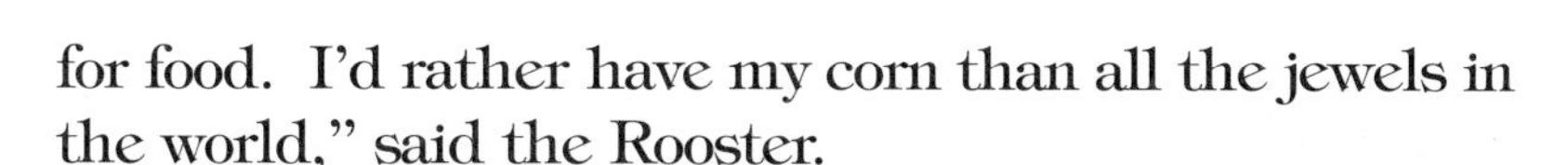

for food. I'd rather have my corn than all the jewels in the world," said the Rooster.

So the Rooster tossed the jewel away, where it was later found by one of the hens. She sold the diamond for $14 million and moved all the hens to a penthouse apartment overlooking Central Park. The Rooster later had to admit to all the other barnyard animals that his hens flew the coop.

Moral: What has value for one is worthless to another.

The Ant and the Grasshopper

One fine summer's day, Ms. Ant and Mr. Grasshopper decided to contribute 50 cents each to buy a lottery ticket together. Sure enough, they picked the winning numbers and became instant millionaires.

Mr. Grasshopper chirped and sang as if he had not a care in the world. He frivolously spent his money on fast cars, fast women and stereo equipment.

Ms. Ant wisely invested her winnings in government security bonds and T-bills.

One day, Mr. Grasshopper called Ms. Ant and said, "Hey, baby, let's go to Monte Carlo together."

Ms. Ant looked at the grasshopper and said, "I see

you do nothing but spend your money like it's going out of style. I, though, am saving my money for the future, and I suggest you do the same."

Months passed. Ms. Ant was happily living off the interest from her investments. Mr. Grasshopper, though, was broke and had charged his Gold Card to the max. After unsuccessfully trying to borrow money from everyone he knew, he had to sell everything he owned to pay his bills.

Moral: It is best to prepare today for the needs of tomorrow.

The Gnat and the Cow

Once there was a silly gnat buzzing around a cow who was sitting with her girlfriends in a bar. The gnat, who thought he was God's greatest gift to bovines, was certain he was irresistible to the beautiful cow. He flew in circles, doing loop-de-loops to attract her attention and admiration. After an hour of acrobatics, however, the cow hadn't even given him the time of day.

Finally, he decided to try a more humble approach, so he settled on the cow's shoulder.

"Pardon me, my dear," he said, "if I am bothering you. If I am, tell me so and I'll leave. By the way, what's your sign?"

"Oh," said the startled cow (who's sign, by the way, was Taurus), "I didn't even notice you were there, so it makes no difference to me whether you go or stay."

With a flick of her tail, the cow gave him the proverbial brush off. The gnat was crushed, so to speak.

Moral: The smaller the mind, the greater the ego.

The Goose with the Golden Eggs

One morning, a stockbroker known as Mr. Farmer was astonished to discover that the goose-shaped water fountain in his posh, Wall Street office was spouting solid gold eggs instead of water.

He seized the precious eggs and locked his office door so no one would know what he was doing. Despite Mrs. Farmer's suggestion that they contact an investment broker, he promptly bought stock in a company he knew would be receiving a multi-million dollar defense contract within a few weeks.

Once the stock price jumped, he sold the stock and invested the profits in a Texas Savings & Loan.

One day he thought, "Why should I wait for these golden eggs to come out of the fountain one at a time? If I smash the fountain, I can get them all at once." So he smashed the fountain, but alas, found no gold inside.

Soon, he was investigated by the SEC and found to be guilty of insider trading. Due to the collapse of the Texas S & L, he was unable to pay his fines and court costs, so he was forced into bankruptcy.

Moral: Those who are greedy for too much sometimes lose all.

The Mice in Council

Once upon a time there was a man named Mr. Katt who worked for a computer accessories company called Mice, Inc. Mr. Katt thought he had quite a way with the ladies that worked at Mice, Inc. One day, the female employees met to discuss how they might handle the unwanted attentions of Mr. Katt.

After much discussion, a young woman stood up and said, "We all know that it is the sly way in which he approaches us that is our greatest danger. I propose we hang a bell around the neck of Mr. Katt. Then we will always know when he is coming, and we will have time to prepare.

At first, the women were very excited about the idea. But then a wise woman asked, "Which one of us will put the bell on Mr. Katt?"

The women of Mice, Inc. looked from one to another, and no one spoke. No one was willing to put the bell around his neck. Mr. Katt was later appointed to the Supreme Court.

Moral: Many things are easier said than done.

The Fox and the Grapes

Once upon a time there was a woman named Miss Fox who had a major crush on one of her co-workers, Mr. Grapes. Mr. Grapes was tall, dark and handsome. And best of all, he wore no ring on his left hand.

Miss Fox used all of her charms to attract the attention of Mr. Grapes. She read magazine articles such as "How to Attract Mr. Right" and "The Right Eye Shadow Can Make You Irresistible". She wore short skirts, sat suggestively on his desk, and asked him out for long lunches to discuss "business". She boasted how they would soon have a juicy relationship.

One day she was walking by the water cooler when

she overheard Mr. Grapes discussing his upcoming wedding. Miss Fox was quite shocked to learn that Mr. Grapes was not only engaged, but was so in love with his fiance that he hadn't even noticed her advances.

When her friends asked how she was doing, Miss Fox whined, "I don't want him anymore. He's not worth my effort, and he obviously can't recognize a good thing when he sees it."

Miss Fox rushed home, canceled her subscriptions and put her "A woman without a man is like a fish without a bicycle" bumper sticker on her car.

Moral: It is easy to despise what one can't have.

The Dog and the Shadow

Mr. Hound was a nice-looking man who was rather bald. Even though Mrs. Hound tried to convince him he was quite handsome without hair, Mr. Hound decided to get a toupee. One day, while taking a walk wearing his toupee, he crossed a bridge over a stream. Looking down, Mr. Hound saw his own shadow in the water. Mistakenly thinking that the reflection was a man with a toupee twice the size of his own, Mr. Hound decided he wanted that toupee, too.

Stretching, he reached toward the man in the stream. At that moment, his own toupee fell off his head and into the stream. It floated away looking not

unlike a drowned rat.

Now Mr. Hound realized at last that what he had seen was nothing but his own shadow. He returned home and told the story to Mrs. Hound, who was really quite happy the toupee had floated away.

Moral: Grasp at the shadow and lose the substance.

The Shepherd who Cried Wolf

Day after day, Miss Shepherd listened to her friends talk incessantly about their husbands and boyfriends. Her friends sounded like sheep, bleating about how wonderful it was to have a man in their lives and how Miss Shepherd needed to find that special someone.

Miss Shepherd longed to find a nice-looking, well-bred, economically-secure man and was tired of feeling left out when her friends discussed their relationships.

One day, Miss Shepherd went to meet her friends for a drink after work. Just to start something, she rushed over to her friends and shouted, "Guess what! I've met the most wonderful man in the world!"

Miss Shepherd continued her intricate lie—that she'd met Mr. Wolff and was engaged to be married.

Unbeknownst to her, a nice-looking, well-bred, economically-secure man was sitting directly behind her. He had seen her before several times and had finally decided to ask her to join him for a drink.

Upon overhearing her stories, however, he simply said, "Your fiance is a lucky man. I was interested in getting to know you better, but since you're engaged, I'll leave." Then, he quickly left the bar before Miss Shepherd could stop him.

Miss Shepherd's chance for a relationship was destroyed, and she left the bar feeling quite sheepish.

Moral: Lies usually come back to haunt you.

The Fox without a Tail

Once upon a time, there was a woman named Mrs. Fox, who had been married for several years. Her husband found out, though, that she was having an affair and they soon divorced.

Ashamed about the loss of her marriage, she hid in her house where no one could see her. She wondered how she could ever face her friends again.

Then one day she had an idea. She hurried to the health club where the other women were gathered and cried loudly, "Look at me, dear friends! You have no idea of the ease and comfort I am enjoying! I've divorced my husband and how wonderful it is to be free of the burden that seemed to always trail behind. And see how it has improved my life! I would like you all to be as carefree as I am. I think you should all divorce your husbands! Get rid of the ball and chain. Then we could all have fun together."

"Mrs. Fox," said one of the wiser women, "tell us, if you had not just gotten a divorce, would you be so ready to encourage us to leave our husbands?"

Moral: Misery loves company.

The Farmer and the Stork

Mr. Farmer (a nice, single gentleman) went out with some friends to a singles bar. There, he saw a group of women out on the dance floor. They were tall, wore very short skirts, and their excessive makeup made them look like cranes. Occasionally, one would leave the bar for a one-night stand with a man she'd just met. Among the cranes, though, was a woman named Miss Stork.

Miss Stork noticed Mr. Farmer sitting at the bar. She approached him and asked him to dance. When Mr. Farmer declined, she noticed the disapproving way in which he looked at her friends who were still out on the dance floor.

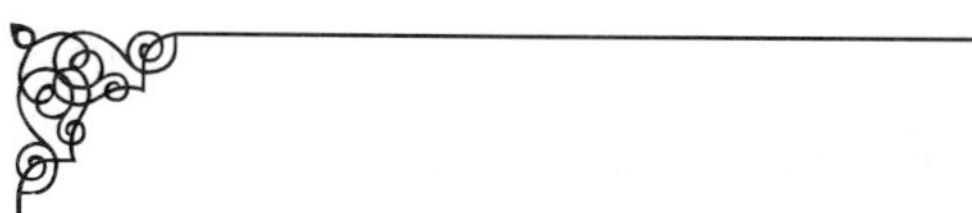

"Oh," she said, "please don't think I'm easy just because the other women are. I am a woman of strong moral character. I ..."

But Mr. Farmer cut her short. "All that you say may be true, but I've seen you with those floozies, and I have every reason to think you are one too."

Moral: Birds of a feather flock together.

The Wolf in Sheep's Clothing

One day, a hungry young employee named Miss Wolf stole into the company where Mrs. Ewe worked as the Assistance Vice President of Finance. The Vice President of Finance had just retired, and Mrs. Ewe was in top consideration for the promotion. Miss Wolf, however, also wanted the position.

Mrs. Ewe developed a plan for the fiscal year, as well as a model to increase profits 18%. Miss Wolf asked Mrs. Ewe if she wanted her to review the proposal before she submitted it. She feigned interest in Mrs. Ewe's work and said she wanted to be a "team player". Mrs. Ewe appreciated this and welcomed her input.

Unfortunately, Miss Wolf stole Mrs. Ewe's ideas and tried to take the credit for it. She bragged about the cost-saving plans she would implement. She wined and dined the president of the company and even tried to turn the rest of the staff against Mrs. Ewe.

The perceptive president, though, recognized the situation, and, due to her hard work and foresight, rewarded Mrs. Ewe with the promotion to Vice President of Finance. Miss Wolf, on the other hand, was fired for unethical conduct.

Moral: Cheaters never win.

The hawk and Pigeons

A man named Mr. Hawkwood long had his eye on a flock of women he called his "pigeons". No matter how hard he tried, he couldn't get any of them to pay any attention to him.

Finally, Mr. Hawkwood decided to use craft and ingenuity to put himself in a more powerful position. From the top of a near-by podium, he called down to his "pigeons": "Why do you prefer a life of constant anxiety, when, if you make me your Senator, I can fight for your rights in Congress?"

The "pigeons", believing the Hawkwood's interest in their welfare to be sincere, elected him to be their

Senator. But as soon as was he elected, he started harassing the women in his employ, demanding they make certain “sacrifices” to him on a regular basis. The women complained, and the Senator from Oregon soon became a national scandal.

Moral: Some sacrifices aren’t worth the price.

Androcles and the Lion

Mr. Lion was a vice president of a major national bank with large accounts, both personal and corporate. Miss Androcles, on the other hand, worked for a small, local bank.

One day, Mr. Lion was on his way to work when he suddenly got a flat tire. It was pouring rain, and he had no jack. The other cars on the freeway were passing him by as he stood on the shoulder, dripping wet.

Miss Androcles was driving down the freeway and recognized Mr. Lion from a banquet she had recently attended. Pulling over, she offered him the use of her jack and a towel (women being prepared for anything.)

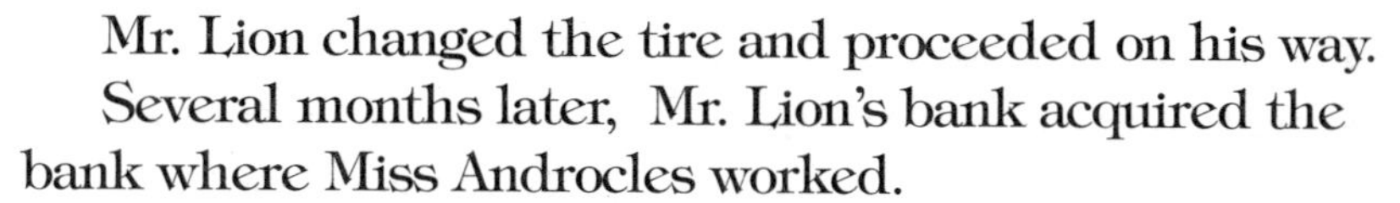

Mr. Lion changed the tire and proceeded on his way.

Several months later, Mr. Lion's bank acquired the bank where Miss Androcles worked.

Miss Androcles' position at the bank was slated to be eliminated. Mr. Lion called her into his office, but seeing the woman who had helped him at the side of the road, persuaded the bank's management to offer her a promotion instead.

Since Miss Androcles was always so well prepared, she became the Vice President of Planning, and lived happily ever after.

Moral: Don't let anybody jack you around.

The Wolf and the Lamb

Once upon a time there was a head of a large company named Mr. Wolf. One morning he spilled his coffee, ran over his wife's cat, bent his seven-iron on the golf course and was rear-ended on his way to work.

When he arrived at the office, he was in an extremely bad mood and decided that firing someone would be just the thing to cheer him up. He walked up and down the aisles looking for a sacrificial lamb.

At last he found the perfect target. A lone employee was working diligently at her desk.

"There's my victim," thought Mr. Wolf gleefully. "But I'll need some excuse for firing the harmless creature."

So he shouted at the lamb, "How dare you sit around doing nothing on company time."

"But you must be mistaken," said the lamb, "I am working very hard right now."

"Don't argue," said Mr. Wolf, "I know you. You are the one who was saying those ugly things about me behind my back last year."

"Oh, no, sir," said the lamb. "I didn't even work here last year."

"Well, if it wasn't you, it was the person who sat at this desk before you. I'm not going to have you talk me out of firing you."

Without hesitation, he fired the poor lamb.

Epilogue: The lamb later sued the company for wrongful termination and was awarded a 1.5 million dollar judgment. Mr. Wolf lost his job, his car insurance dropped him and his wife divorced him, citing excessive stress over the loss of her cat. All in all, it was a very bad day.

Moral: The meek shall inherit the company.

The Aunt and the Dove

A young woman named Dove knew her aunt had recovered from her divorce and was ready to test the waters of the dating scene. Not wanting her to get in over her head, Dove thought it would be nice to introduce her aunt to her boss, Mr. Tern, who was about the same age as her aunt and was also recently divorced.

The aunt and Mr. Tern hit it off immediately. Glad to be out of the dating pool, they set their sights on the distant shores of Hawaii and ran off together for a two-week vacation.

When they returned, the aunt learned that Dove's

boyfriend had dumped her. Dove was quite dejected. After Dove finished her tale, her aunt said, "Never fear, my dear. The wonderful man you introduced me to has a son just about your age. What do you say we double-date next Friday night?"

Dove and the young Mr. Tern also hit it off instantly, and the following spring Dove and her aunt were married to the two Mr. Terns in a double ceremony.

Moral: One good tern deserves another.

The Mischievous Dog

Reverend Dawg once had a large, fundamentalist congregation. He preached from his pulpit each Sunday on the evils of gluttony and the sins of the flesh. His sermons were simulcast on cable television across the country. Often, his wife would join him at the altar to greet his flock. People around the world would gather to see him and to donate their savings to his church.

One day, Reverend Dawg's secretary unexpectedly called a press conference. Then and there, she announced to the world that she and the Reverend had

been having a torrid love affair. The Reverend had paid for her posh, ocean-front apartment for their trysts. She was now confessing her sins to clear her conscience.

But there was more to the tale. The money donated by the Reverend's congregation paid for the apartment hide-away and a fancy house for he and his wife. They were living in the lap of luxury, and, of course, the income was tax exempt.

At first, he denied all of the allegations. When he realized the extent of the free media coverage, he tried to take advantage of the situation. He was confident

that his flock would not desert him and the law would not prosecute him, being next to God and all.

Tearfully, he confessed his sins to the world and garnered top news ratings. With mascara streaming down her face, his wife pledged to love and support him and to stand by her man.

The law, not being influenced by his relationship to God, thought financial fraud was pretty serious and threw Reverend Dawg in jail. He was released on parole five years later, but found his wife standing by a new man. She divorced him and remarried quickly.

Reverend Dawg hoped to cash in on notoriety and regain his flock, but they had moved on to another shepherd. He couldn't pull the wool over their eyes.

Moral: To be widely known is not necessarily to be admired.

The Donkeys Eating Thistles

It was dinnertime, and the Donkey family was on their way to a wonderful French restaurant for dinner. Mr. and Mrs. Donkey were all dressed up and the kids wore their best clothes.

When they arrived at the restaurant, the menu looked delicious, at least to Mr. and Mrs. Donkey. It was a veritable smorgasbord of delicacies. The two parents placed their orders, then the waiter turned to the children for their choices.

"We want hot dogs," said the children, who were not at all interested in the fancy food. "Hot dogs taste better than this stuff on the menu. That junk probably

tastes like thistles."

The kids proceeded to create quite a scene, and the family had to leave the restaurant without ever getting their escargot.

Moral: Get a baby-sitter.

The Stag and the Pool

Buck was getting ready for a blind date. His friends had arranged dinner with a lady they promised to be the woman of his dreams. He studied his reflection in the window of the local pool hall and thought, "My, how terrific my broad shoulders look. My weight-lifting is paying off. I could be a body double in the movies!"

But then he sighed as he thought, "If only I weren't so bald." He went home, searched through his closet and found a toupee his friends had given him as a joke years ago. Putting it on his head, he said, "Wow! This makes me look young and handsome. I'm sure to impress the girl of my dreams tonight!"

He left for the restaurant to meet his date. They had a lovely evening together and seemed to have a lot in common. She truly was the girl of his dreams.

When the evening ended she said to him, "Buck, I've really enjoyed meeting you. I had a nice time, but you're just not quite what I was looking for. I expected someone older and more distinguished. You are so young and athletic, and deserve someone who will love you as you are." With that, she turned and left without waiting for a response, leaving Buck the bill.

Moral: Too often we despise that which we should value most.

The Fox and the Crow

Mr. Crow, an advertising agent, was entertaining a potential new client, a cheese manufacturer, at a local karaoke bar.

As the two men talked, a woman entered the bar. She was also an advertising agent, but worked for Mr. Crow's competitor and was competing for the account. She approached the table where they were talking and said, "Mr. Crow, how nice to see you!"

"Why, Miss Fox," said Mr. Crow, "what a nice surprise!" The client asked Miss Fox to join them, and Mr. Crow couldn't figure out a polite way to exclude her. So Miss Fox joined the table.

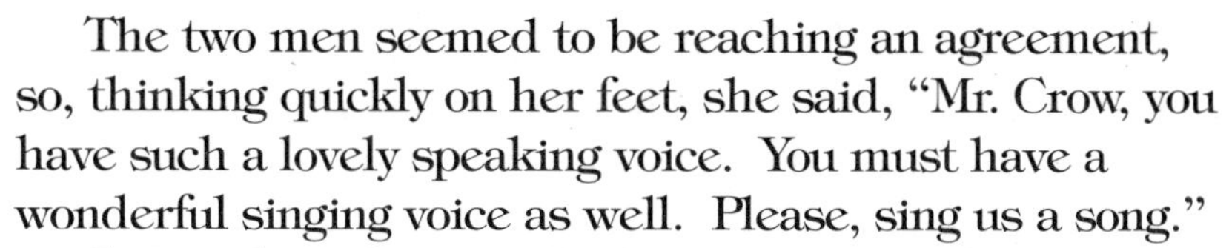

The two men seemed to be reaching an agreement, so, thinking quickly on her feet, she said, "Mr. Crow, you have such a lovely speaking voice. You must have a wonderful singing voice as well. Please, sing us a song."

So Mr. Crow, being gullible, went up to the stage and started his own personal rendition of "Feelings".

While he was on stage, Miss Fox slyly gave her pitch to the potential client. The client loved her ideas and signed the contract on the spot.

Mr. Crow was aghast to later discover he had lost the deal. He couldn't believe she'd do such a cheesy thing.

Moral: Never trust those who praise you falsely.

The Milkman and his Pail

Once upon a time, a man who worked as a sales rep for a dairy was on his way to give a presentation to a large grocery store chain. Certain he would get the account, he was already thinking of ways to spend his commission. He dreamt of a trip to the Caribbean, where he would get a tan and meet "chicks" in slinky bikinis. He'd also buy himself a new red convertible.

Unfortunately, due to his lack of attention, his old car hit a large pothole in the road. His milk samples spilled all over his car, and he got a flat tire as well.

By the time he finished changing the tire, he was not only late, but was quite dirty as well.

"You're finally here," said the client, "but where are your samples?"

"I spilled them," he said, "but don't worry, I can have more here tomorrow."

"Not good enough," said the client. "I'm afraid I'll be purchasing all of our milk from your competitor."

So the man returned to his old car and drove back to his office where he had to explain to his boss how he lost the account. Completely dejected, he mourned the loss of his trip, his car, his chicks in bikinis and his job.

Moral: Don't cry over spilled milk because you counted your chickens before they were hatched.

Jupiter and the Bee

Long ago, there was a queen bee who had stored an excellent supply of delicious honey. She wished to offer the honey as a gift to Jupiter, so she flew off to Mount Olympus to deliver it.

Jupiter was so impressed with the gift that he promised the bee anything she wanted.

"Oh, powerful Jupiter," she said. "Give me a stinger so strong that if anyone approaches to steal my honey, I can kill him on the spot."

Jupiter was angry and shocked that the bee would avenge the theft of her honey in such a way. "Your wish will be granted. You shall have your stinger; however, when you attack anyone who takes your honey, the wound shall be fatal to you as well. Your life shall go with your stinger. You will have to decide if the honey is worth more than your life, honey."

Moral: To bee or not to bee, that is the question.

The Country Mouse and the Town Mouse

Once upon a time, there were two cousins who shared the last name of Mouse. One of the cousins was a plain, but nice girl with a good personality who lived in the country. The other was a beautiful model who lived in the big city.

One day, the country cousin invited her city cousin out for a day in the country. All day long, she cooked and cleaned, preparing for the arrival of her cousin.

When the city cousin arrived, she turned up her perky little button nose at the food, the house, and the lack of entertaining men in the country. "How is it, my cousin, you can endure the boredom of living like a nun

in a convent? You can't really prefer this dullness to the excitement of life in the city!"

The city cousin continued, saying, "You're wasting your time out here. There's more to life than guys with pickup trucks! Come with me to the city and I'll show you the time of your life."

So the country mouse decided to join her cousin in the city. It was late when they arrived and almost midnight before they reached the penthouse apartment.

The country cousin wanted to prepare for bed, but the city cousin said, "Not a chance. The evening is young and it's time to party. But first, you need some decent clothes and some make-up."

So the city cousin dressed the country cousin as if she was a doll. She gave her a tight, short, black leather dress, fishnet stockings and 4" heels. Then, the two left for a nightclub.

The country cousin wobbled into the nightclub and looked around in amazement. Before her, she saw a wonderful spread of beefcakes — and the food didn't look too bad either. The city cousin played hostess to her country cousin, bringing her drinks and introducing her to the city men in the nightclub.

Just as the country cousin was beginning to feel comfortable in her 4" heels, police burst into the club.

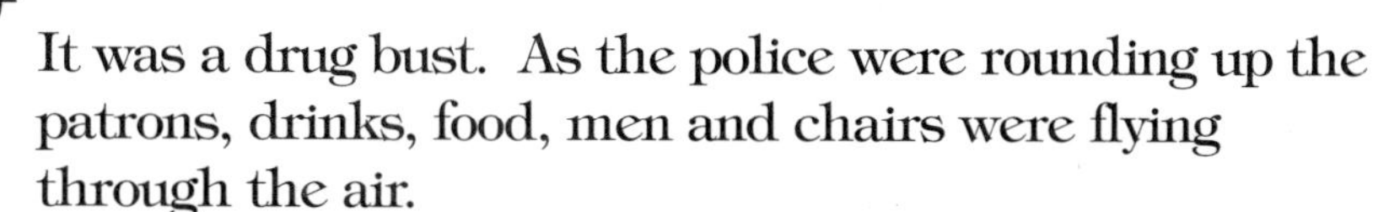

It was a drug bust. As the police were rounding up the patrons, drinks, food, men and chairs were flying through the air.

The city cousin quickly dragged her country cousin out before the police could question them. The cousins hailed a cab and returned to the townhouse. When they arrived, the country mouse said, “This is a fine way to live for people who like it. But give me the peace and quiet of the country. I’ve decided I like men who drive pickup trucks.”

Moral: Stick with what you know.

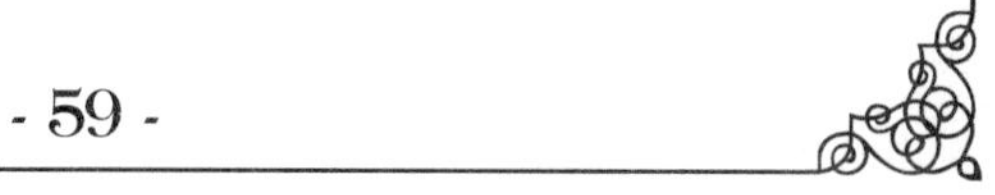

The Goatherd and the Goats

Mr. Goatherd was a happily married man until a blonde bombshell named Bambi entered his life. He fell (he thought) head over hooves in love with the blonde. He abandoned his wife and four children to spend the rest of his life with his new-found love.

Unfortunately, the new-found love had other ideas. After accepting his expensive gifts and fancy jewelry, she moved on to greener (richer) pastures.

Mr. Goatherd, seeing the errors of his ways, called his wife pleading, "Please forgive me and take me back."

But Mrs. Goatherd was much too wise for idle talk. She filed for divorce and won a mighty hefty alimony

settlement. Mr. Goatherd realized she wasn't kidding and paid promptly every month for the rest of his life.

Moral: The grass is not always greener on the other side of the fence.

The Eagles, the Wildcats and the Sows

Three families, the Eagles, the Wildcats and the Sows, lived in a building that had been converted into ritzy condos. The Eagles lived on top, the Wildcats lived on the second floor and the Sows lived on the first floor.

One day, Mrs. Wildcat visited Mrs. Eagle. "That Sow woman," she said, "chases anything wearing pants. While her husband is at work, she even chases the mailman. I'm going to keep a close eye on my husband, and I suggest you do the same."

A little while later, Mrs. Wildcat visited Mrs. Sow. "That Mrs. Eagle," she said, "is after your husband. She said she wanted to wrap her claws around him."

Needless to say, this caused quite a rift between Mrs. Sow and Mrs. Eagle. For weeks, the two women didn't speak to each other. One day, the two women noticed that Mrs. Wildcat hadn't come home from the grocery store. Mrs. Wildcat had abandoned her family and had run away with the mailman. Mr. Wildcat enlisted the help of both Mrs. Eagle and Mrs. Sow to care for his children while he was at work.

They discovered they had been victims of idle gossip. "How catty," the women thought.

Moral: Beware a gossip's tale.

The Lion and his Three Counselors

Mr. Lyon, the CEO of a Fortune 500 software company, was in an irritable mood. That morning, his wife had told him that his breath was most unpleasant. After doing considerable roaring to prove he was in charge, he summoned three of his Vice Presidents.

First, he called Ms. Sheep. "Ms. Sheep," he said, opening his mouth widely, "do I have bad breath?"

Thinking her boss wanted an honest answer, she gave it. The CEO then bit off her head for being a fool.

Next, he called Mr. Wolff and asked him the same question. Mr. Wolff, after noticing the subdued manner of Ms. Sheep, said, "Why, Mr. Lyon, your breath is as sweet as a summer's breeze." Before he could finish, Mr. Lyon ripped his head off for being a flatterer.

Finally, Mr. Lyon called Ms. Fox and put the question to her. Ms. Fox quickly assessed the situation, then coughed lightly. "Mr. Lyon," she said, "I have such a head cold that I cannot smell a thing."

Moral: During trying times, a wise woman always says nothing.

The Fir and the Bramble

As they jogged around the indoor track in their gym, Mr. Fir and Ms. Bramble were discussing their respective jobs. Mr. Fir, who was a mid-level manager for an airplane manufacturer, was bragging about the benefits and perks he received working for a large corporation.

His boasting annoyed Ms. Bramble, who said, "In your position, I would not put on such airs."

Mr. Fir haughtily replied, "How can you, a struggling, self-employed woman, understand the feelings of a young, upwardly mobile executive marching his way to the top?"

"Just wait," said Ms. Bramble, "until your company downsizes the next time. Then I'll bet you'll wish you were self-employed, too."

Moral: Better self-employed than unemployed.

The Man and his Two Women

A middle-aged man, whose hair had begun to turn gray, was married to a woman slightly older than himself. He also had a younger girlfriend on the side. His wife, ashamed to be married to a man younger than herself, made a point whenever he was asleep, to pull out some of his black hairs.

His younger girlfriend, on the other hand, not wishing to be seen with an old man, was equally zealous in removing every gray hair she could find.

Thus, it came to pass that between both his wife and his mistress, he soon had not a hair left on his head.

Moral: Having affairs makes men go bald.

Venus and the Cat

Once upon a time, there was a woman named Miss Katt. She had met and fallen madly in love with a Harvard-educated lawyer with political aspirations. But she, a waitress in a coffee shop, knew she could never hold her own in his circle of friends.

So Miss Katt decided to attend Venus' Finishing School. There, she learned proper, lady-like manners and the art of conversation. Her schooling paid off, for her lawyer fell madly in love with her.

He asked her to be his wife, and they soon married. Mr. Venus, however, had seen the wedding announcement in the newspaper. Wanting to know if she

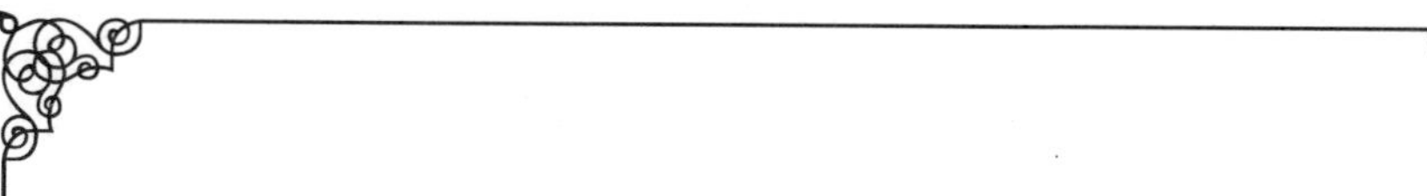

was able to pull off the illusion of upper class, he attended the reception. He approached the bride saying, "I'd like two eggs over easy and a cup of Java."

The woman turned to go to the kitchen, then realized her faux paw. Mr. Venus, finding it humorous that she had revealed her true nature, told her husband the entire story.

Mr. Venus was last seen being chased by a woman in a wedding dress and wielding a kitchen knife while shouting obscenities.

Moral: Don't mess with a bride on her wedding day.

The Farmer and the Snake

Miss Farmer had dated her new gentlemen friend a couple of times when he came to her with a tale of great woe. Not only had he lost his job, but his apartment was being converted into condos and he had nowhere to live.

She took compassion on him, and despite the advice of her friends, took him home to live with her. "He's a snake," her friends all said, "he's just using you."

But Miss Farmer believed them to be wrong. The man quickly adjusted to his new life and spent his days at home watching cable TV. While Miss Farmer worked late into the evening to support them both, he went to the local bar for beers.

There, he met a beautiful, rich widow who could support him in grander style. Without so much as leaving a note, he took all his belongings from Miss Farmer's apartment and ran off with the widow.

Miss Farmer was deeply hurt by his actions. "Oh," she cried to her friends, "what an awful scumbag he turned out to be."

"We told you so," said all of her friends.

Moral: Never get rattled by a snake.

The Oaks and the Reeds

Once upon a time there were two families who lived next door to each other, the Oaks and the Reeds. Each family had children who attended the same school.

The Oaks raised their children to follow strict rules and never let their children make any decisions on their own. The Reeds, however, gave their children guidelines to follow and allowed their kids to make their own decisions within the guidelines.

One day, Mrs. Oak went to have tea with Mrs. Reed. "Donna," Mrs. Oaks said, "my children (whom she affectionately referred to as her 'little acorns') are teenagers now and they're driving me nuts. They want

me to make every decision for them, from what they're going to wear in the morning to where to go to college. What shall I do?"

Mrs. Reed replied, "It is the rigid way you dealt with your children that has brought you to this point. Bending the rules on occasion would have given them the chance to make decisions on their own."

Moral: ***Flexibility can strengthen family trees.***

The Two Potts

A woman and her new husband once lived in the same town as the husband's mother. Both women shared the last name of Potts.

Soon after her son and daughter-in-law were married, the older Mrs. Potts wanted her son and daughter-in-law to move in with her to live "happily ever after." The mother-in-law came over for dinner one night, and noticed her son's favorite soup was warming on the stove.

Knowing her son liked extra salt on his food, she added some to the soup. She did not know, however, that her daughter-in-law had already salted the soup.

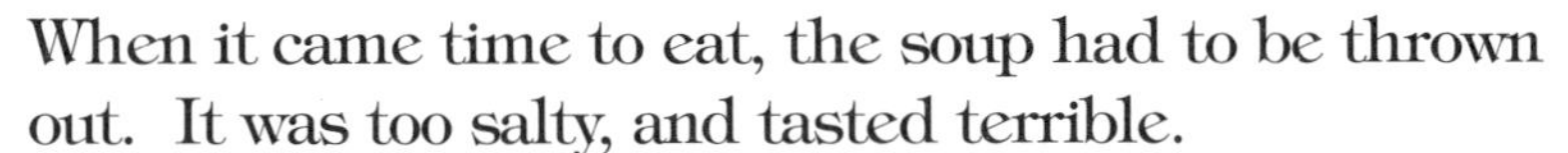

When it came time to eat, the soup had to be thrown out. It was too salty, and tasted terrible.

The elder woman said, “Come live with me, and I’ll take care of your every need. I’ll cook just the way my son likes, since you, of course, won’t be able to.”

The younger Mrs. Potts wasn’t terribly fond of this idea, and said to the older Mrs. Potts, “You’re very kind, but that’s just what I’m afraid of. The two of us living under the same roof would be sure to clash, and banging pots make a terrible racket. We’ll avoid stormy waters and keep our own house.”

Moral: ***Too many cooks spoil the soup.***

The Wolf and the Shepherd

Mr. Wolf came to work for the company owned by Mr. Shepherd. He had previously worked for Mr. Shepherd's competitor, so Mr. Shepherd was a little worried about his intentions.

Mr. Shepherd kept a close eye on Mr. Wolf as he developed relationships with both new and existing customers. As time went by, Mr. Shepherd came to believe that Mr. Wolf truly had his new employer's best interests at heart.

One day, Mr. Shepherd turned over all of the customer information to Mr. Wolf, then left for a two-week cruise to the Bahamas.

While he was gone, Mr. Wolf stole the client files and returned to the competitor, bringing with him many of Mr. Shepherd's clients.

Mr. Shepherd returned from his vacation to discover he'd been fleeced.

Moral: Once a competitor, always a competitor.

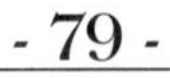

The Travellers and the Bear

Two travellers were in a Chicago bar discussing football. After bad-mouthing the local team, they turned around only to discover a Bear behind them. He was an angry Bear. He didn't like being spoken about in a derogatory manner, so the Bear picked up a chair and threatened to fight the two men if they didn't recant their statements.

One of the travellers was prepared to defend himself, even though the Bear was three times his size. Then, he saw his partner had dived behind the bar to hide.

Figuring the Bear would go away and leave him alone, the first man pretended to faint dead away from fear. The Bear leaned over and whispered to the man, then, disgusted with the behavior of both men, left the bar in a huff.

When the second traveller came out from behind the bar, he asked, "What did that Bear say to you when he whispered in your ear?"

"Two things," replied the first traveller. "Don't trust a friend who deserts you when trouble comes."

"What was the second?" asked the other traveller.

"Move to Cleveland," he replied.

Moral: Don't go out on the field unless you're willing to play.

The Wolf and the Shepherds

Miss Wolf stood outside the doorway of a publicly-funded, prestigious military college. Inside, she knew male wolf cadets obtained an education she was denied the right to have, simply because she was a she-wolf.

Overseeing the college was a stuffy board of directors (all male) known as the "Shepherds". They had proud careers in the military, but were short-sighted when it came to women, whom they called the "fairer sex".

Miss Wolf decided to stand up for her rights and challenged the Shepherds. "I'm just as good as the male wolf cadets you have here, and I want the same opportunities they have."

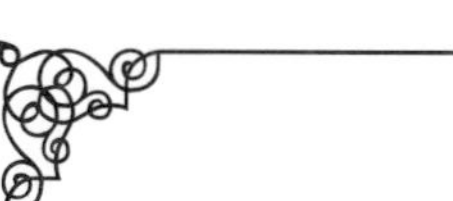

The Shepherds laughed at her, so she went to court. After a couple of Supreme Court Justices ruled the college had to let her in, she was finally allowed the same opportunity as the male wolves.

Sadly, due to the mental strain of her treatment by the college and the male wolves, she decided to return to the forest. Even though other male wolves also chose to leave, the remaining wolf cadets labeled her as "weak" and celebrated her departure, in the process showing their contempt for the Supreme Court and the laws of their country.

Moral: Wolf cadets always follow older wolves.

The Vain Crow

Once upon a time there was a crow who wanted to be the most beautiful crow in the country. She entered beauty contests and soon became the representative from her state at the Miss Crow America pageant.

She purchased the finest of clothes and strutted around town like a peacock. "I'm going to be Miss Crow America, but I'll always remember you little people," she said with her beak stuck in the air.

As the pageant organizing committee was reviewing Miss Crow's credentials, they noticed several discrepancies in her application. After further research, the committee discovered that Miss Crow was not a Phi

Birda Kappa as she had stated on her application, and, even worse, she had posed for Playcrow!

The committee stripped her of her state title and sent her packing. The bedraggled Miss Crow, sadder but wiser, returned to her home town. When she arrived, she would have been happy to be accepted by her neighbors; however, they would have nothing to do with her.

Moral: Pretending to be a peacock when you're a crow can lead to fowl results.

The Old Woman and the Physician

An old woman, who had become blind, summoned a physician. "Since you are my doctor," she said, "I would like to see if you can restore my eyesight."

So the physician ran some tests and determined the cause of the problem. He referred her to a specialist, who was not on the list of "preferred providers" covered by her insurance plan.

The specialist examined the woman and agreed to treat her provided she pay her medical bills after she was cured.

After a time, the malady disappeared, and the woman regained her sight.

When she saw the medical bills, she submitted the forms to her insurance company and to Medicare. Due to the number of forms she had to fill out, though, she once again became blind, and the whole process started all over again.

Moral: *The medical forms resulting from the cure can be as bad as the disease.*

The Horse and the Laden Ass

A family named Farmer once had two cars. One car was nice and new, and had plenty of leg room. They referred to this car as the "Horse". Their other car, a van, was older and was not as reliable. They often referred to the van as the "Ass".

One day, Mrs. Farmer had to drive the carpool for her son's baseball team practice. "There are so many children," she said to her husband. "Could you take some in your car?" she asked.

Her husband replied, "Not in the nice car. Take them all in the van."

So the entire baseball team piled into the van. A

couple of miles later, the van broke down. Calling her husband from her car phone, Mrs. Farmer informed him of the situation and told him to come pick up the kids.

So Mr. Farmer loaded the kids into his car. Only having enough seat belts for four kids at a time, he needed to make several trips to the practice field. The kids tracked mud all over the car, and the leather seats were riddled with cleat marks.

Mrs. Farmer was picked up by Triple-A and was driven home, where she took a long bubble bath while waiting for her husband and kids to return.

Moral: Revenge really can be sweet.

The Lion and the Mouse

Mrs. Lyon was the Vice President of Finance for a major national company. One day, she was walking around her department and noticed one of her employees, Mrs. Mouse, was doing her nails and talking to her husband on the telephone.

Mrs. Lyon called Mrs. Mouse into her office and said, "Unless you want to broaden your employment horizons, stop doing personal business during company time."

"Oh, please," said Mrs. Mouse. "Don't fire me. I promise I'll work harder. Forgive me this time, and I won't forget it. A day may come when I can repay your kindness by protecting your job."

Mrs. Lyon was amused by the thought that this lowly employee might be of assistance in this way, so she decided to give her another chance.

Not long afterward, Mrs. Lyon found out that internal auditors were coming to review the company's financial statements. She worked late into the night entering data into the computer so she would be prepared for the audit the next morning.

When she came in the next morning, though, she discovered that she had neglected to save any of her data from the night before. "Woe is me," she cried. "Whatever shall I do?"

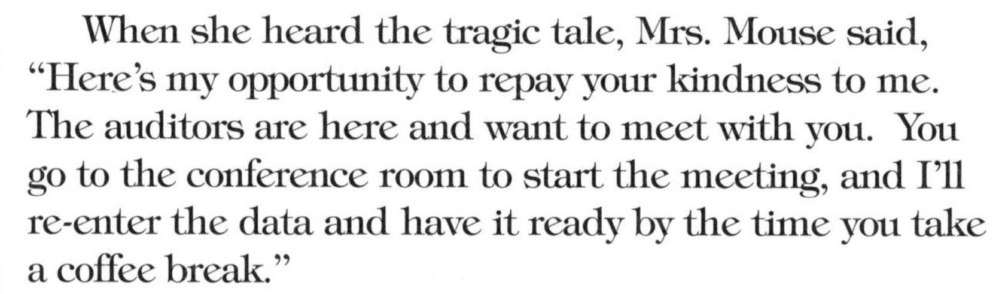

When she heard the tragic tale, Mrs. Mouse said, "Here's my opportunity to repay your kindness to me. The auditors are here and want to meet with you. You go to the conference room to start the meeting, and I'll re-enter the data and have it ready by the time you take a coffee break."

So Mrs. Lyon was able to present the financial reports to the auditors after all. The financial data was in such good order she was promoted to CFO. Mrs. Mouse was promoted to become her Executive Assistant.

Moral: Data saved is data earned.

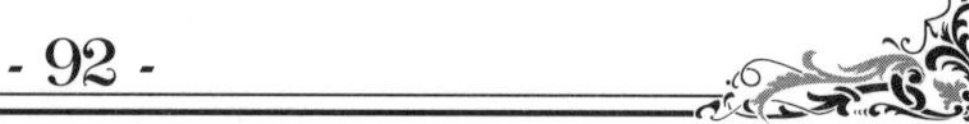

The Travellers and the Hatchet

Two women who were on vacation in Hawaii were walking on the beach. Ahead of them on the beach lay a gorgeous, tan, hunk of a man. His hair glistened like the blade of a hatchet in the sunlight.

"Look what I found," said the first traveller. "A potential date for the evening."

"Don't say 'look at what I found,' say 'look what we found.' I think I might be interested in him as well," said the second woman.

So the two women watched and waited until he woke up. Once he woke up, however, and began to speak, it was clear to the women that the guy was a real jerk.

"We've found a real jerk," said the first woman.

"Don't say 'we found a real jerk', say 'I found a real jerk!'"

Moral: She who will not allow her friends to share in the prize must not expect her to share in the spoils.

The Two Crabs

Mrs. Crab and her twenty-one year old daughter were both home one Friday evening. The younger Crab was getting ready to go out for the evening. Before she could leave the house, though, her mother stopped her.

"You can't go out dressed like that!" she said. "Your skirt is much too short and that blouse is practically see-through."

"But Mom," her daughter replied. "You dressed like this when you were my age. I've seen pictures of your first date with Dad."

"Precisely my point, my dear." said Mrs. Crab, thinking of her husband, Buster.

After a moment's thought, the young Miss Crab realized the implications of the situation, and went upstairs to change.

Moral: Do as I say, not as I do.

The Donkey in the Lion's Skin

The suave Donkey (sporting gold chains, a hairy chest, platform shoes and polyester suit) thought he was no longer cool (meaning he wasn't scoring with the "babes") and decided to pursue a more macho image. Soon, he came upon the skin of a lion.

He thought to himself, "Dressed as a lion, I can scare away all the other animals and find myself a cute little filly." So he ditched his other clothes and put on the lion skin. Then he went cruising for some action in the forest. All of the other animals ran and hid when they saw him coming.

Finally, the Donkey came upon a Fox. "Hey, babe,

what do you think of these threads?" asked the Donkey.

The Fox looked him over, then she replied, "Clothes only make the man until he opens his mouth."

Moral: An Ass in fine clothing is still an Ass.

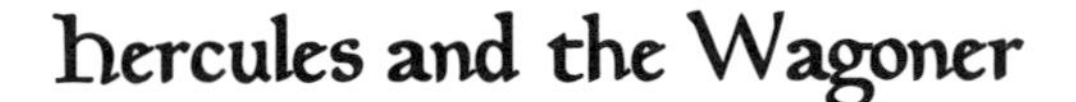

Hercules and the Wagoner

Mrs. Hercules was quietly taking a bubble bath and reading a trashy romance novel when her young son, Wagoner, suddenly bellowed from the kitchen.

"Mommm," he shouted. "I can't do my math homework. Come help me."

"Have you even tried yet?" sighed Mrs. Hercules.

"It's way too hard, and besides, the teacher hates me anyway," he replied.

"But have you tried yet?" she asked again.

"Well, no. But it's not fair I have to do all this homework all by myself," he said. "If you help me, I can watch television the rest of the night."

Mrs. Hercules replied, "Try to work through your homework by yourself, and don't ask for help unless you have tried first." With that, she went back to reading her trashy romance novel.

Then the phone rang. "It's for you, Mom," he said.

Moral: Kids and phones are common denominators when it comes to hot bath interruptions.

The Fox and the Woodcutter

Miss Fox and Miss Woodcutter were roommates. One Friday night they were both home, when there came a knock on the door.

Miss Fox, thinking it might be her soon-to-be-ex-boyfriend, asked Miss Woodcutter to answer the door. "If it's Hunter," she said, "tell him I'm not here."

When Miss Woodcutter answered the door, there she found the boyfriend. "Is my girlfriend here?" he asked.

"No," replied Miss. Woodcutter in a voice loud enough for her roommate to hear. Making sure she was behind the door so Miss Fox couldn't see her, she winked and pointed in toward the bedroom.

Hunter, thinking the woman was making a pass at him said, "Sorry, lady, I'm a one-woman man," and promptly left.

When Miss Fox came out, Miss Woodcutter said, "I got rid of him. Aren't you going to thank me?"

Miss Fox replied, "I saw you winking and pointing at the bedroom. Either you were trying to tell him I was here, or you were making a pass at him. Either way, I'm not going to thank you."

Moral: There is as much mischief in a wink as in a word.

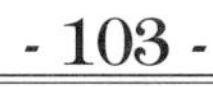

The Fisherman and the Fish

At a family gathering, Mr. Fish had just a little more beer than he needed. Thinking he could entertain the crowd, he got his wife and kids together and formed an impromptu singing group called "The Fisherman and the Fish."

With his wife and kids behind him to provide the back-up vocals, he began doing his best rendition of "Midnight Train to Georgia." Everyone at the gathering soon discovered Mr. Fish couldn't sing.

When the rest of his family was supposed to chime in with "bop-bop-sha-bop," there was nothing but silence. Mortified, he slunk off the stage.

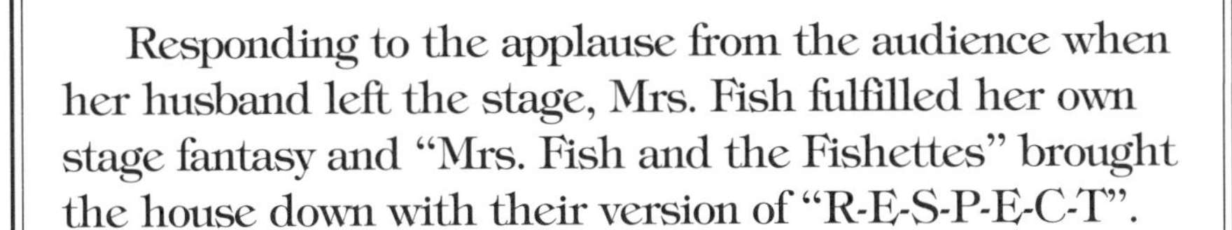

Responding to the applause from the audience when her husband left the stage, Mrs. Fish fulfilled her own stage fantasy and "Mrs. Fish and the Fishettes" brought the house down with their version of "R-E-S-P-E-C-T".

Moral: Don't succumb to temptation unless you have the voice to be one.

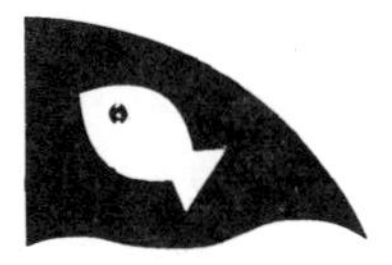

The Horse and the Lion

Ms. Lyon was sitting in her office feeling sorry for herself. Business had not been very good the past week. Suddenly, the phone rang. It was a man from Horse Industries offering a major defense contract. The two agreed to meet.

The next day, Ms. Lyon and the representative from Horse Industries met. Ms. Lyon was salivating at the thought of landing such a lucrative contract. The two discussed the scope of the project and the payment for Ms. Lyon's services. Ms. Lyon licked her chops.

The gentleman from Horse Industries leaned over and said, "I can guarantee you this contract, if only you'll pay me 10% of your profits." There was a sickening silence, and Ms. Lyon felt as if a hoof had kicked her in the nose.

"Never," she said. "I want to win this contract on my own merits."

As the man from Horse Industries left, the last thing Ms. Lyon heard was the whinny of his laughter.

Moral: Don't horse around with kickbacks.

The Ladd and the Filberts

Mrs. Ladd put her hand into a jar which contained a goodly quantity of chocolate-covered filbert nuts. She clutched as many as her fist could possibly hold. But, when she tried to pull her hand out, the narrowness of the neck of the jar prevented her from doing so.

Unwilling to lose any of the chocolates, but yet unable to pull her hand out of the jar, Mrs. Ladd burst into tears and cracked open the jar by breaking it on the kitchen counter. This allowed her direct access to all of the chocolate.

Her husband, realizing a sign of PMS when he saw it, promptly went to the store for more chocolate.

Moral: Never, ever come between a woman and her chocolate.

The Squeaky Wheel

Ms. Wheel worked for a software company called MicroOxen. The company was about to release the new version of its transportation management software called Wagons '95.

Many of the MicroOxen employees worked day and night preparing the software for its release.

Ms. Wheel, although only indirectly involved in the project, whined and complained about the long hours and severe stress. Each morning, she would tell her co-workers how late she worked the night before, and how early she had arrived that morning. Because she was so selfish, she didn't realize her co-workers were working

even longer hours.

Her boss, finally tired of hearing her complaints, had her transferred out to a division specializing in automobile service and repair software. There, she worked less hours and received less pay. Meanwhile, the Wagons '95 team all received substantial bonuses.

Moral: The squeaky wheel gets greased.

The Ass Goes Dating

Mr. Mule was once dating two women at the same time. (No, it wasn't a threesome; the women didn't know about each other.) He knew, eventually, he'd have to choose between the women, but he couldn't bring himself to make a decision.

One day, he was out with Miss Rabbit, when Miss Bunny walked into the restaurant. Seeing her honey with another woman, Miss Bunny became quite upset. Miss Rabbit was none too thrilled to discover Mr. Mule was two-timing her as well.

The women stormed out of the restaurant, leaving Mr. Mule alone at the table with nothing but the bill.

The two women, while comparing notes over wine coolers at a local tavern, decided to start a self-help group called CADD (Chicks Against Dual Dating).

Moral: Don't split hares.

The Wild Boar and the Fox

Miss Boar was busily primping herself in the mirror. She was dressed to the nines, had applied her make-up "just so" and was spraying on her favorite perfume when her roommate, Miss Fox asked, "Why are you wasting your time in this manner. There aren't going to be any men at the Tupperware party we're going to tonight."

"True enough," replied Miss Boar, "but when the opportunity presents itself, I shall have something else to do than worry about how I look."

Moral: A good scout is always prepared.

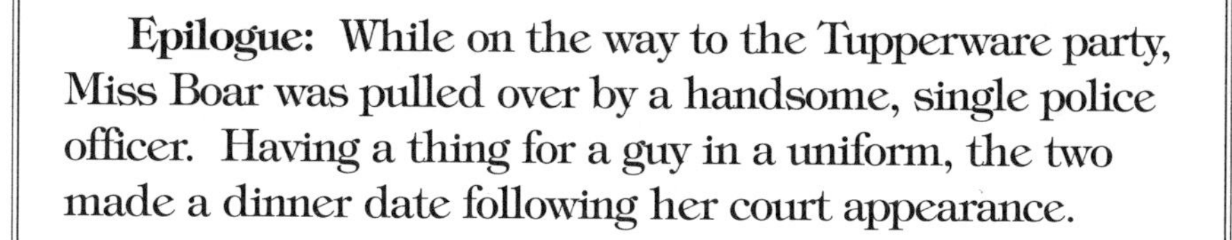

Epilogue: While on the way to the Tupperware party, Miss Boar was pulled over by a handsome, single police officer. Having a thing for a guy in a uniform, the two made a dinner date following her court appearance.

The Beasts, the Birds and the Bats

Once upon a time, Mr. Batt was elected to the Senate. His country had a two-party electoral system. One party was known as the "Beasts", and the other was known as the "Birds".

For a long while, a battle ensued over who would control the Senate. Mr. Batt, wanting to enjoy the best of both worlds, tried to be aloof and remain neutral.

In due course, the Beasts gained control of the Senate, and Mr. Batt flew to join them in their rejoicing.

Soon, though, the mood of the country switched. A President who was for the Birds was elected, and the Batt decided to switch parties.

Unfortunately, Mr. Batt had some nasty dealings regarding election rule violations, so neither party would claim him as a member.

Moral: He who plays both sides against the middle gets voted out of office.

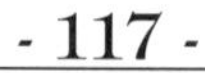

The Mouse and the Basket

Mr. Mouse and his wife went to the home of Mr. and Mrs. Basket for Thanksgiving dinner. During the meal, Mr. Mouse stuffed himself with multiple helpings of everything on the table.

"Argggh," came a cry from the bathroom. "What's the matter?" asked the spouse of Mr. Mouse.

"I ate too much," moaned Mr. Mouse, "and I can't get my pants buttoned up."

Mrs. Mouse retorted, "I told you not to take that fourth helping of stuffing. You'll just have to stay in there until you can button your pants. Call a cab when you can. I'm going home."

With that, the mortified Mrs. Mouse moseyed home without Mr. Mouse.

Mr. Mouse, deciding it didn't matter that his pants wouldn't button, sat down to watch a football game and drink beer with Mr. Basket, who had by this time unbuttoned his pants, too.

Moral: Boys will be boys.

The Lark and the Young Ones

In the early spring, Mr. and Mrs. Lark were both working hard to provide a good home for their children, who also made convenient tax deductions.

On April 13th, Mr. Lark turned to his wife and said, "Taxes are due soon. I must get my buddy to help me complete the forms and file the return." But at the end of the day, the tax forms were still sitting inside the manila envelope.

On April 14th, Mr. Lark turned to his wife and said, "Taxes are due soon. I must get my brother to help me complete the forms and file the return." But at the end of the day, the tax forms were still sitting inside the

manila envelope.

On April 15th, Mr. Lark began to panic. Mr. Lark turned to his wife and said "I asked my buddy for help, and I asked my brother for help. I am going to do these taxes myself." So he locked himself in his study and began working on his taxes.

Mrs. Lark, not wanting the children to be exposed to nasty language at such a young age, took the children to the zoo. Later that night, at 11:55 pm, she drove to the Post Office to mail the extension form she had picked up "just in case."

Moral: If you want it done, hire an accountant.

The Wind and the Sun

A dispute once arose between two friends over who could get a date with a handsome man the fastest. There seemed to be no way to settle the issue, but then a nice, handsome young man moved into their apartment building.

"This is our chance," said Miss Wind, "to prove who is right. Whichever of us can make a date with that man shall be the winner. I'll go first."

So Miss Wind put on her sexiest dress, highest heels and most expensive perfume. Then, she went to introduce herself to the new neighbor. She came on like a tornado, but the harder she pressed, the more

the man resisted. At last, she gave up in disgust. "He must be gay," she thought.

Then Miss Sun tried her approach. She made a batch of cookies and went to visit the neighbor. As he felt her charm and warmth (and ate the cookies), he invited her out for dinner the next night.

Miss Sun not only won the bet, but fell madly in love with the man, who was definitely *not* gay.

Moral: The easiest way to a man's heart is through his stomach.

The Two Deer

One day, Mrs. Deer decided to go on a diet. She enlisted the help of her husband, John, and asked him to remind her about her diet if she started to eat something unhealthy.

After dinner, the little deers were in bed, and Mr. and Mrs. Deer were watching television. Going to the kitchen, Mrs. Deer brought back a piece of chocolate cake for her husband and a small sliver for herself.

When her husband reminded her about her diet, she replied, "I know, dear, it's such a small piece though. I'm rewarding myself after eating so well today."

She finished her cake in two bites, while her

husband still had plenty to eat. So she went back to the kitchen for another small slice, then another and another. When her husband reminded her again about her diet, she replied that the trips to the kitchen counted as exercise.

Moral 1: Chocolate cake eaten one sliver at a time has no calories.

Moral 2: A woman can justify anything.

The Rat Race

Once there was an election year, and two Congressmen were competing for the Rat party nomination for President. Representative Oldt thought he was the best choice to lead the party to victory. Senator Pineapple, however, thought he would make the best president.

To their constituents, both denied they were even interested in the nomination. Rather, they claimed they were in Congress working for the good of the people.

When it came time to file for candidacy, however, both men were at the front of the line. Although Representative Oldt's wife didn't think he should run,

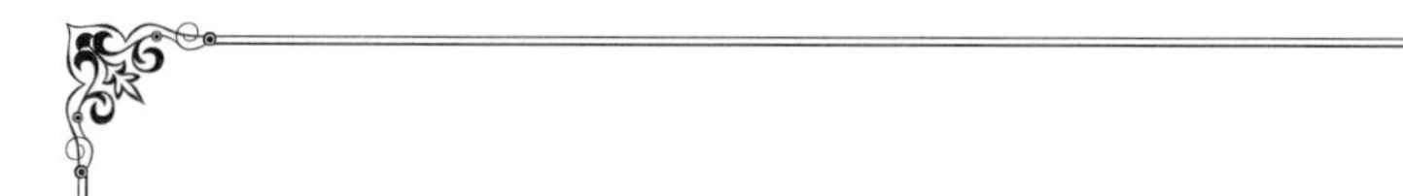

he figured he'd toss his towel into the ring anyway.

With that, the press began their feeding frenzy and tried to uncover the skeletons in the closets of both men. The men were more than happy to point fingers at each other, and at the incumbent from the other party. In no time, the race was on.

Moral: Whoever wins a rat race is still a rat.

The Mountains in Labor

Once upon a time, Mr. Mountain was greatly agitated. His wife, Mrs. Mountain, was in the hospital delivery room about to give birth to their first child.

Loud groans and noises were heard, and crowds of people came from all parts to see what was the matter. They were quite surprised to discover that Mr. Mountain was the one making all the noise.

Mrs. Mountain calmly practiced her breathing exercises as she had learned in Lamaze class, while her husband ran around the hospital shouting, "We need more towels, we need hot water."

Finally, at the crucial moment when his first child

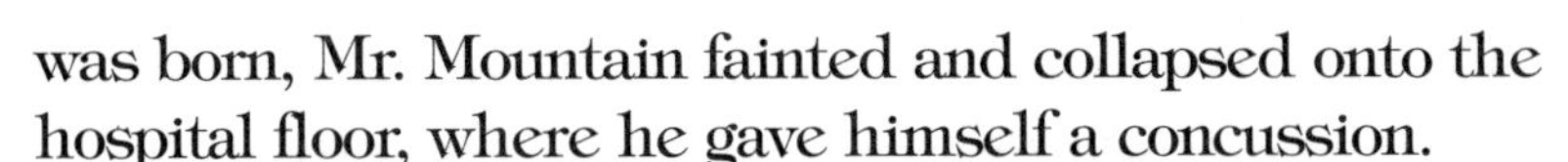

was born, Mr. Mountain fainted and collapsed onto the hospital floor, where he gave himself a concussion.

Mrs. Mountain, although exhausted from the delivery, was up and about in just a few hours. Her husband, however, was in x-ray.

Mr. Mountain was kept in the hospital for several days for observation. Mrs. Mountain and the baby, Rocky, were discharged the next day because of insurance limitations for hospital stays after delivery.

Moral: Insurance companies often try to make molehills out of mountains.

The Porcupine and the Moles

Mr. and Mrs. Mole were relaxing in their cave one day, peacefully enjoying their retirement and the fact that all of their children were leading their own lives.

Just as they were planning their next trip in their motorhome, there came a knock at the door. When he opened the door, Mr. Mole was quite surprised to find his son, affectionately known as "Porky" standing outside with several suitcases.

"Dad," he said, "I've lost my job, and the little woman kicked me out just because I had a fling with a cute little chipmunk. I have to move back in with you and Mom for awhile."

The Moles, generous parents that they were, consented to their son's request and allowed him to move back home. The cave was small, and every time the parents moved, they tripped over their son, who was content to sit and watch TV instead of look for a job.

Finally, Mr. and Mrs. Mole decided the cave wasn't big enough for everyone, so they packed their belongings into the motorhome and headed to Arizona for the winter. There, they discovered many other parents escaping from their children as well.

Moral: Sometimes children are like bad pennies— they keep turning up.

The Perfect Houseguest

Kay Lin desperately wanted to be rich and famous. Having no talent, however, posed quite a problem for her in the pursuit of her goal.

To solve the problem, Kay Lin travelled in elite social circles, making sure to be seen with actors, singers and ex-sports stars.

Kay Lin soon made an art form of being the "perfect houseguest" at the residence of one of her new-found friends. She was constantly in high demand and was thrilled to be living in the lap of luxury (free of charge, of course).

Kay enjoyed the lifestyles of the rich and famous, and

was often seen playing golf or going for fast food with her benefactors.

One day, one of her benefactors' residence was the scene of a crime. When she was interviewed by the police, then ultimately called to testify, her only response to questions was "Um ... I can't remember."

She was, however, approached by several tabloids wanting to print the stories she couldn't remember. Finally, she had what she wanted—fame, recognition and a chance for her own late-night talk show.

Moral: Talent is in the eyes of the beholder.

The Lioness and the Cubs

Once upon a time, Mrs. Lion had to drop one of her children at a scout meeting, take another to track practice, and finish some work she brought home from the office.

Asking one of the other cub scout's mothers to bring her son back to the den when finished, she decided not to stay for the meeting. Instead, she finished her chauffeuring, then went home to finish her work.

When her young cub came home, he told his mother he had nominated her to head the annual fund raising drive, which began at the end of summer. Being the only nominee not present, her approval was unanimous.

Moral: Pride goeth before the Fall.

Epilogue: After her son excitedly sprang the news of her unanimous election, Mom explained the facts of life: Never nominate Mom for a committee unless she's in the room at the time.

The Flat Knight

Miss Knight was observing herself in the mirror one day and realized that her bust was quite flat. To make herself more attractive (and to attract Mr. Right), she decided she needed a more voluptuous figure.

Off she went to the department store. After Miss Knight tried on every brand of push-up bra, the clerk finally said in frustration, "Honey, you just don't have anything to push up in the first place."

Miss Knight returned home. She had only an hour to get ready to go out with her friends. In desperation, she decided to stuff her bra with tissue. Then, she put on her slinkiest black dress and went out for the night.

As Miss Knight and her friends were sitting in the bar, one of them asked for a tissue. Forgetting what her tissues were for, Miss Knight reached into her dress for one, and all of them on one side fell out. As the tissues floated to the floor, Miss Knight's companions began to laugh. It was definitely a Knight to remember.

As she turned to run from the bar, she bumped into a rich, handsome attorney. "My dear," said Mr. Wright, "you are beautiful the way you are. Please have dinner with me tonight." So Miss Knight joined him, and a wonderful relationship had begun.

Moral: Don't put all your hopes into one chest.

Mercury and the Woodsman

Miss Woodsman once made a chocolate cake for her church social. Although not the best cook in the world, she gave it her best shot. The cake, however, was slightly lopsided and looked a little strange.

While she was standing at the dessert table, single and handsome Mr. Mercury walked up.

Pointing at the most beautiful cake on the table, Mr. Mercury asked, "Miss Woodsman, did you make this delicious-looking cake?"

"Alas, I wish I did," replied Miss Woodsman sadly.

Pointing at another beautifully decorated cake, he said, "Perhaps this masterpiece is yours."

"No," she said. "I'm afraid it's not," as she looked at her lopsided creation.

"This one?" he asked, pointing at the dismal failure.

"Yes," she sighed, lowering her head shamefully.

"You are an honest and good woman," he said. "Are you free Saturday night?"

Miss Woodsman graciously accepted the gentleman's dinner invitation.

Miss Barracuda, overhearing their conversation, pointed to a scrumptious chocolate cake and exclaimed, "Oh, Mr. Mercury, I made this cake and I'm free on Friday night."

Mr. Mercury replied, “Not so fast, lady. This seems a little fishy. My mother made that cake. And another thing, I don’t date women who lie about something as important as chocolate.

Moral: Honesty can make the Mercury rise.

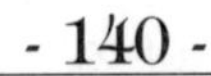

The Quack Frog

A politician, emerging from the mud of Texas like a frog from a swamp, announced to all the voters that he could cure the problems of the country. He planned to run the country like he ran his vast business empire. So, Mr. Parrot declared his candidacy for President with an independent party.

Interested to see what all the croaking was about, the voters gathered around, and the politician, more pumped up than ever, bellowed, "Come and see! I am the greatest businessman in all the world."

Then, he was interrupted by the bray of a donkey and the trumpet of an elephant.

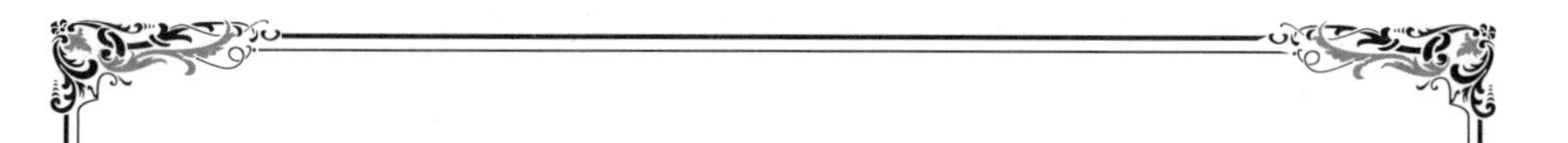

"How dare you try to steal our votes," they said.

So the frog challenged the donkey and the elephant to a debate, where the entire country discovered that his eyes bugged out and he had a croaky, weak voice. Eventually, the donkey who won the election, and the frog returned to business, with the voters laughing behind his back.

Moral: Politics ain't all it's quacked up to be.

The Donkey and the Database

Once upon a time, Mr. Donkey, a business executive, needed some assistance in developing a computer database for his company.

Contacting one of his vendors, Mr. Donkey arranged for the vendor to create the database.

The vendor labored long and hard on the project. When the work was almost finished, Mr. Donkey terminated the agreement with the vendor. He then proceeded to complete the database himself and took credit for the entire project.

If anything went wrong, though, Mr. Donkey claimed that the vendor was at fault. Finally, when the project was completed, the vendor happily moved on to work with other clients.

Moral: Once an ass, always an ass.

The Raven and the Swan

Once upon a time, there was a raven who became a big rock star. Although he earned a lot of money, he became dissatisfied with his lot. He was especially unhappy whenever he saw the swans floating gracefully about in a nearby pool.

"I want to be just like that swan," said the raven, pointing at a white bird.

The raven was determined to do something to make himself look more like a swan. So the raven saw a doctor who specialized in feather-bleaching. His plumage was lightened, but it just didn't turn out the same color as the swan's. The raven told everyone he

had developed a rare feather disease to cover his embarrassment and retired in seclusion.

Moral: Be happy with what you are.

The Mouse in her house

Mrs. Mouse was preparing for a special weekend with her husband. She sent the children to her parents for the weekend and came home early from work early on Friday.

She cooked her husband's favorite dinner, put on a silk negligee, lit candles and had soft music playing in the background.

When she heard a noise at the front door, she opened the door expecting to see her husband. To her shock and dismay, she instead saw her in-laws.

"What are you doing in your nightgown at this hour? Are you sick? And why are the candles lit? Is your power out?" asked her mother-in-law in one breath.

"Well, we're here to see Mickey," said the mother-in-law. "We came for a surprise visit this weekend."

The younger Mrs. Mouse was indeed surprised. Thinking fast on her feet, she replied, "Oh, yes, I have a bad flu. And there was a terrible windstorm. The power will be out for hours. Go to a motel in town."

So the relatives left, and Mrs. Mouse told her husband that his parents were in town…the next day.

Moral: The best laid plans of mice and men are often interrupted by in-laws.

The Three Tradesmen

One day, Miss Tiger discovered all the computers down in her office. As head of the department, it were her responsibility to get the computers working again.

First, she called her hardware vendor and explained the situation.

"It's a software problem," said the hardware vendor.

So she called her software support line and, once again, explained the predicament.

"It's a network problem," said the software vendor.

Sensing that a pattern was developing, Miss Tiger called the network vendor.

"It's a hardware problem," replied the network vendor.

Miss Tiger considered her alternatives. Her first thought was to throw the file server out the 12th floor window, but not wanting to injure anyone below, she decided against it.

Next, she decided to tackle the problem herself. After several references to the manuals, she solved the problem. She then called the three vendors and cancelled their contracts.

Moral: If you byte off more than you can chew, try reading the manual.

The Monkey and the Dolphin

Miss Dolphin was waiting for her friends at a hotel restaurant. Mr. Monkey, seeing an opportunity to get a date, asked if he could join her.

Miss Dolphin, noting he was nicely dressed and very polite, allowed him to take a seat.

As they chatted, Mr. Monkey asked her where she was from. When she replied, “Seattle,” Mr. Monkey said, “Why, so am I. I attended the University of Washington.” (He hadn’t, but had read that by establishing a common bond made it was easier to pick up chicks.)

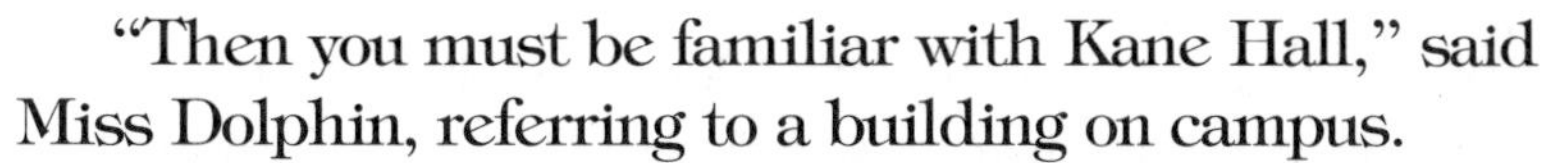

"Then you must be familiar with Kane Hall," said Miss Dolphin, referring to a building on campus.

"Of course," said Mr. Monkey, guessing that Kane Hall was the name of a distinguished professor, "He was one of my favorite instructors."

Disgusted by such an obvious falsehood, Miss Dolphin left the fool and joined her friends, who were observing from a nearby table.

Moral: Don't monkey around with the truth.

The Lion and the Clicker

One evening, Mr. and Mrs. Lion were having a disagreement over what to watch on TV. Mrs. Lion's favorite show was premiering the same night as the baseball playoffs and the VCR was broken.

Knowing that whoever controlled the remote control also controlled the television, Mr. Lion pounced on the device. He figured that with his superior strength, he could fend off the "little woman".

Mrs. Lion, having anticipated such a development, had earlier removed the batteries from the remote control. Mr. Lion, knowing when he was beaten, agreed to watch the game over at his buddy's house.

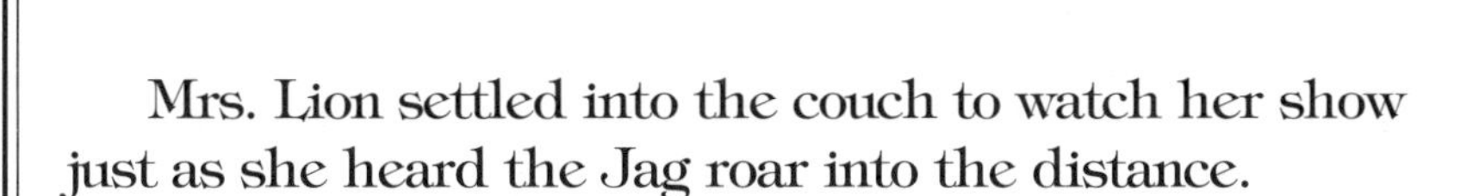

Mrs. Lion settled into the couch to watch her show just as she heard the Jag roar into the distance.

Moral: Brains always wins over brawn.

The Worker Ants

Mr. and Mrs. Ant were expecting their first child. Mr. Ant, to make sure he could be reached at any moment, set up voice mail at work, and had it automatically forwarded to a pager which was in turn connected to his computer so he could receive text messages. Then, he bought a cellular phone with a car lighter adapter so he could even be reached on the road.

When the crucial moment arrived, Mrs. Ant called her husband at work. She was connected to his voice mail, where she left a message that she was calling a cab and going to the hospital. Unfortunately, Mr. Ant's pager battery had run down, so he didn't receive the call that was forwarded by voice mail.

After several minutes, Mrs. Ant tried to call her husband on the cellular phone. Unfortunately, Mr. Ant had left the car's lights on, which drained the battery, which meant his cell-phone didn't work.

When Mr. Ant finally got the message, he sped to the hospital. There, he proudly discovered he was the father of a baby boy named Adam.

Moral: Buy extra batteries.

The Bundle of Sticks

Once upon a time there was a basketball team known as the Steers. The team had many talented players, several of whom were sports and media stars.

Despite the lack of teamwork because each player wanted to be the biggest star, the team won several games and advanced to the playoffs.

Each player dreamed of the endorsements he might land. "Oh," each thought, "the glamour and fame I could have. And I can make more money than the other players by endorsing soda, cars and underwear.

Finally, it came time for the last game of the finals. Each player tried to show up the others. Instead of

working as a team, the game became a series of one-man shows. The team lost miserably, and the promise of individual endorsements quickly faded.

Moral: Dreams of careers leading to underwear endorsements may be brief.

The Donkey and the Lap Dog

Miss Donkey and her coworker, Miss Hound, once had a crush on the same man from the office.

Miss Donkey was a dedicated worker, who had responsibility and respect within the organization.

Miss Hound, on the other hand, was always flitting about, flirting with the gentlemen by the water cooler.

One day, Miss Donkey noticed Miss Hound and the handsome man going out to lunch together. Naturally, she began to feel sorry for herself. It galled her to see the man fall for such behavior.

Thinking that if she behaved the same way as Miss Hound she might get a lunch invitation as well, she

tried her hand at flirting.

The next day, she wore high heels, a tight skirt and lots of make-up. When she saw her target at the water cooler, she tried her best to attract his attention.

Instead of responding to her, the man turned and walked away. After he left, he turned to one of his colleagues and said, “It’s too bad she’s so flighty—I thought she was more professional and sophisticated. I was planning on asking her out, until now.”

Moral: If he doesn’t ask you, ask him.

A man who had two daughters sent them off to college so they could learn to lead productive lives as professional women.

After college the two daughters spent several years working their way up their respective corporate ladders. One became a successful banker; the other a successful real estate broker.

One day, the father went to visit the daughter who was a banker. "How fares it with you, daughter?" he asked her.

"Very well," she replied. "I have everything I want. I have but one wish. Interest rates are rising at a steady

pace, and I hope it continues, for my department is more profitable than ever."

Later, the father visited the daughter who was a real estate broker. "And how is everything with you?" he asked her.

"There is nothing that I lack, but I do have one wish—I hope interest rates fall soon because my business will thrive again."

"Alas," thought the father, "I wish I knew what to wish for."

Moral: You can't please everybody.

The Crow and his Show

Once upon a time, a crow decided to host his own talk show. In front of all the crows, he'd discuss the latest sensational news and hot celebrity gossip.

His shows were often controversial; during one he received a broken beak as the result of being hit by a branch thrown by one of his guests.

After several successful seasons, the crow decided to host a special exposé. A world renowned squirrel purportedly had a large cache of gold nuts hidden in a secret vault in a tree. The crow found the tree and decided to open the vault. In front of all his viewers, he broke into the tree, only to discover an empty trunk.

Quite embarrassed, he returned to his tabloid journalism, and stuck to uncovering nasty exposés on various other forest animals.

Moral: Talk shows are for the birds.

The Man and his Dog

Once upon a time, there was a man who had a dog named Baroque. Baroque was a manly dog and cavorted with the many lady dogs in the neighborhood. Tired of caring for puppies, the man decided a trip to the veterinarian was in order.

Baroque, though, had other ideas. As soon as the man opened the door to take him to the vet, Baroque bolted out of the house and ran away. The man searched the neighborhood and finally found a dog hiding in his neighbor's back yard. Unfortunately, the man mistook the neighbor's dog for his own and took his neighbor's dog to the vet. When he returned home he found his dog waiting on the front porch. He returned the second dog to its home, where he met his neighbor, a profesional mud wrestler. The mud wrestler was less than pleased to learn that his dog had been altered.

Moral: If it ain't Baroque, don't fix it.

OTHER TITLES BY GREAT QUOTATIONS

201 Best Things Ever Said
A Lifetime of Love
A Light Heart Lives Long
A Teacher Is Better Than Two Books
The ABC's of Parenting
As A Cat Thinketh
The Best of Friends
The Birthday Astrologer
Cheatnotes On Life
Chicken Soup
Don't Deliberate . . . Litigate
Fantastic Father, Dependable Dad
For Mother–A Bouquet of Sentiments
Global Wisdom
Golden Years, Golden Words
Growing Up In TOYLAND
Happiness Is Found Along The Way
Heal The World
Hollywords
Hooked on Golf
I'm Not Over The Hill
In Celebration of Women
Inspirations
Interior Design For Idiots
Let's Talk Decorating
Life's Simple Pleasures
Money For Nothing, Tips For Free
Motivating Quotes For Motivated People
Mrs. Aesop's Fables
Mrs. Murphy's Laws
Mrs. Webster's Dictionary
Mrs. Webster's Guide To Business
Parenting 101
Real Estate Agents and Their
  Dirty Little Tricks
Reflections
Romantic Rhapsody
The Secret Language of Men
The Secret Language of Women
The Sports Page
Some Things Never Change
TeenAge Of Insanity
Thanks From The Heart
Things You'll Learn, If You Live
  Long Enough
Women On Men

GREAT QUOTATIONS PUBLISHING COMPANY
1967 Quincy Court
Glendale Heights, IL 60139-2045
Phone (708) 582-2800
Fax (708) 582-2813